WITHDRAWN

12 GREAT TIPS ON
WRITING A SPEECH

by Catherine Elisabeth Shipp

www.12StoryLibrary.com

Copyright © 2017 by Peterson Publishing Company, North Mankato, MN 56003. All rights reserved. No part of this book may be reproduced or utilized in any form or by any means without written permission from the publisher.

12-Story Library is an imprint of Peterson Publishing Company and Press Room Editions.

Produced for 12-Story Library by Red Line Editorial

Photographs ©: pixdeluxe/iStockphoto, cover, 1; Library of Congress, 4, 22; ajt/Shutterstock Images, 5; Olesya Feketa/Shutterstock Images, 6; Housh/Shutterstock Images, 7; Alina Solovyova-Vincent/iStockphoto, 8, 27, 28; Photo Africa/Shutterstock Images, 9; Beth Swanson/Shutterstock Images, 11; Image Point Fr/Shutterstock Images, 12; Atomazul/Shutterstock Images, 13; Jan_S/Shutterstock Images, 14; Christopher Futcher/iStockphoto, 15; LuckyBusiness/iStockphoto, 16; chatchawanak/Shutterstock Images, 17; Fuse/Thinkstock, 18, 29; Susan Chiang/iStockphoto, 19; Steve Debenport/iStockphoto, 20; Viorika/iStockphoto, 23; Dragon Images/Shutterstock Images, 24; Corepics VOF/Shutterstock Images, 25; Michael Jung/iStockphoto, 26

Library of Congress Cataloging-in-Publication Data
Names: Shipp, Catherine Elisabeth, 1969- author.
Title: 12 great tips on writing a speech / by Catherine Elisabeth Shipp.
Other titles: Twelve great tips on writing a speech
Description: Mankato, MN : 12-Story Library, 2017. | Series: Great tips on writing | Includes bibliographical references and index.
Identifiers: LCCN 2016002325 (print) | LCCN 2016004535 (ebook) | ISBN 9781632352774 (library bound : alk. paper) | ISBN 9781632353276 (pbk. : alk. paper) | ISBN 9781621434450 (hosted ebook)
Subjects: LCSH: Speechwriting--Juvenile literature.
Classification: LCC PN4142 .S53 2016 (print) | LCC PN4142 (ebook) | DDC 808.5--dc23
LC record available at http://lccn.loc.gov/2016002325

Printed in the United States of America
Mankato, MN
May, 2016

Access free, up-to-date content on this topic plus a full digital version of this book. Scan the QR code on page 31 or use your school's login at 12StoryLibrary.com.

Table of Contents

Know What You're Talking About

What do Martin Luther King Jr. and Abraham Lincoln have in common? Besides being great leaders, both gave speeches that are still famous today. Speeches are usually written down. They are always spoken to an audience. Presenting a speech aloud helps the speaker engage with the audience.

People give speeches for many reasons. Speeches can be used to give information, share stories, or persuade listeners. Speeches can also be used to motivate or bring about action.

No matter why you are giving a speech, you need to know your subject inside and out. To do this, you need to research. Books, magazines, and the Internet are great resources for gathering information. You can also interview people. As you research, write information on notecards or type it into a computer. Organize the information into general ideas. Later, you will structure it into the main points of your speech.

When you research, look for information that is new and surprising. Find

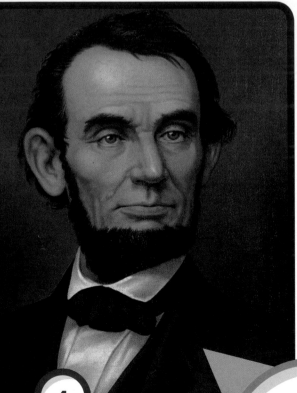

Abraham Lincoln

NOTE-TAKING

An example of taking notes for research:

Why is a longer recess a good idea for kids?

- Kids stay active.
- Kids stay healthy.
- Kids' brains are more ready to learn.

Why is a longer recess not a good idea for kids?

- Kids will get too hyper and not be able to focus.
- It provides too much time for bullying or injuries.
- Kids need to spend more time learning in the classroom.

information that goes against your initial thoughts. This way, you will be able to show listeners that you've thought about all sides of an issue. Don't ignore information that goes against what you think you will be writing about. Instead, find ways to use the information to make your views stronger.

Quick Tips

- Speeches can give information, share stories, or persuade listeners.
- Find information through research.
- Opposing information can help make your speech better.
- Take notes on what you find.

Check out what others have written about your topic.

5

2

Stay Simple

When you write a speech, you want to make sure to focus on a single subject. Engaging the listeners will be easier if people can concentrate on one issue. For example, let's say you want to write about school lunch. You think older students should be served more food than younger students. If your speech includes the history of how apples are grown, you will probably lose your listeners. Instead, your speech should tell listeners key points about why you believe what you do.

Listeners may lose interest in a speech that is not focused.

Keep your speech's structure simple.

Another way to engage listeners more is to structure your speech in a simple way.

Organize your speech with a beginning, a middle, and an end, just like other forms of writing. The beginning of your speech prepares listeners for what they'll be listening for. The middle of your speech is the longest part. It includes details that add to the main points. The end ties together all of your points. It gives listeners a reason to keep thinking about what you have said.

TRY IT OUT

Think of something you would like to tell others about. Write your point, what you most want your listeners to understand, in just one sentence.

Quick Tips

- Focus on one subject in your speech.
- Organize your speech into a beginning, a middle, and an end.
- Give your speech structure to help listeners follow your thoughts.

3

Consider Your Audience and Tone

When you give a speech, you will be in front of an audience. Maybe your listeners are your class of 25 students. Maybe it's in front of your school of 500 students. No matter the size of the audience, your speech is what will connect you with your listeners.

Think about your audience before you begin writing. Giving a speech in front of 25 of your fellow students is different from a speech you would give in front of 25 parents. Giving a speech in front of 25 people who agree with your ideas is different from a speech you would give in

Think about whom you will give your speech to as you write.

front of 25 people who don't agree with you.

After you've determined who will be in your audience, decide on the tone of your speech. The tone expresses an emotion, such as funny or serious. Tone includes how you write the speech as well as how the listeners understand it. For example, you might have a joke you want to tell because you think it is a good introduction to your subject. But the joke might make listeners think you do not take the subject seriously. The tone of your speech also includes other things. What you wear helps set a tone. Your actions, such as hand gestures, help set the tone. Where you give your speech— standing in front of a lectern, or sitting at your desk—also adds to the speech's tone. It is important to keep your tone the same so that you give your listeners a clear message.

Quick Tips

- Determine who will be in your audience.
- Your words, actions, and appearance contribute to your tone.
- Keep your tone the same.

Hand movements help set the tone of your speech.

Hook the Listener

The beginning of the speech is one of the most important parts. If listeners do not pay attention from the start, they may not understand your message clearly. It is important to grab your listeners' attention right away.

One way you can engage your listeners is to start with a question. This gets your listeners to think about how they would respond. If you are writing a speech about the importance of good manners, you could start the speech like this: "What do the words *please*, *thank you*, *you're welcome*, and *excuse me* have in common? That's right. Nothing." A surprising answer to your own question will make listeners want to hear more.

Another way to hook the listeners is to lead with an anecdote. An anecdote is a short story that highlights what you'll be talking about. If you're writing about good manners, you could start the speech like this: "Once there was a little boy who was very rude at lunch. He was so rude that he got sent to the principal. That little boy was me." Again, this opening surprises listeners and makes them interested in what you have to say.

A different way to hook your listeners is to start with a statistic. For example, you could start your speech like this: "When 1,000 people filled out a questionnaire 12 years ago, 25 percent thought that others had poor manners. The same

TRY IT OUT

After you decide on your subject, write three different ways to start your speech. Write a question, an anecdote, and a statistic.

The opening of a speech makes people curious to learn more.

study filled out 10 years later showed 45 percent of people thought others had poor manners." Opening in this way makes listeners wonder what changed over the years. They hope you can tell them.

Quick Tips

- Grab your audience's attention from the start.
- Make your listeners curious.
- Try starting your speech with a question, an anecdote, or a statistic.

STARTING YOUR SPEECH

The following are three ways to start a speech on the subject of recess:

Question: Do we want our country to be half full of couch potatoes?

Anecdote: A student named Ben went to class after his 10-minute recess. He was so restless that he couldn't focus on the test and got half of the questions wrong.

Statistic: According to *Student Magazine*, 48 percent of children who don't get a 30-minute recess every day cannot catch their breath after one minute of running.

Choose Your Words Carefully

It is important to choose your words carefully in all types of communication. When you will be saying the words aloud, it is even more important. There are a number of things you need to think about when choosing how to present your information. First, avoid words you don't know how to say or have a hard time saying. During your speech, you will most likely stumble on unfamiliar words. Even after practicing your speech, you may be nervous. You may forget how to say them. For example, the word *otorhinolaryngologist* looks fancy and important. But it is probably not the easiest word to say. Instead, you could write "ear, nose, and throat doctor" and say the entire phrase with ease.

On a similar note, avoid words you think listeners will not understand. Take, for example, the ear, nose, and throat doctor. A lot of people may not understand the longer term.

Otorhinolaryngologist is a fancy word, but ear, nose, and throat doctor is easier for people to understand.

When people don't understand what you are saying, they may stop listening.

In addition, avoid words you can't say in order. Think of tongue twisters, such as "She sells seashells by the seashore." If you write words in an order that you notice makes you stumble, write the words in a different order or change the words themselves.

Another important way you can choose your words carefully is to write using active verbs. Active verbs put the emphasis on doing instead of being. For example, this sentence has a passive verb: "The president *was transported* by helicopter." This sentence has an active verb: "The helicopter *transported* the president."

Good verbs give a sense of action.

Quick Tips

- Avoid words you can't say easily.
- Avoid unfamiliar words.
- Avoid words that are hard to say in order.
- Use active verbs.

WORD CHOICE IN SPEECHES

The crossed-out words in the following paragraph show changes in word choice. Can you tell why the changes were made?

According to *Student Magazine,* 48 percent of children who don't get a 30-minute recess every day cannot catch their breath after one minute of running. ~~Pulmonologists~~ Doctors who are experts on ~~alveoli, the thoracic cavity, and the pleura~~ lungs suggest exercise as one way to stay fit. A longer recess is one way to exercise. Therefore, students should ~~have~~ participate in a longer recess at school.

13

Guide the Listener

You've structured your speech into a beginning, a middle, and an end. As you move from one part of your speech to the next, it is important to use transitions. Transitions are words that help the listener understand how thoughts and ideas relate to one another. They help guide the listener through your speech.

You can transition in a speech in different ways. One way is to use cardinal numbers, such as *one*, *two*, and *three*. Another choice is to use ordinal numbers, such as *first*, *second*, and *third*. You can also use order words: *first*, *next*, *then*, *last*, *finally*. Each of these techniques helps listeners understand how your thoughts connect.

Transitions are also useful to show how your thoughts relate to others' ideas. For example, you might give an opposing view in your speech. You could follow it up by

Transitions connect one idea to another.

Think about what emotions you want listeners to feel.

saying, "Even though my opponent believes this, I have found it to be false because . . ." This transition makes it clear that you disagree. Your listeners don't need to do as much work to understand your position.

In many forms of writing, the most emotional part of the piece is near the end. This is often called the "turning point." But in a speech, the structure is different. The hook is when you want listeners to feel strong emotions. The middle can have more details to explain your point. The end needs a second emotional draw. Ending with emotion will help your ideas stay with your listeners after your speech is done.

TRY IT OUT

How do you want listeners to feel during your speech? For example, do you start with something gloomy and end with optimism? Write down different possibilities.

Quick Tips

- Organize your speech to guide the listener.
- Use transitions.
- Appeal to listeners' emotions in the beginning and end of your speech.

Repeat the Important Points

As you write your speech, remember to repeat yourself. You've probably been taught not to repeat yourself in other forms of writing. Speeches are different. Your listeners will remember your thoughts and ideas if you say them several times.

You do not need to say the same exact sentences in order to repeat yourself. You can instead repeat key words or phrases. For example, if you're writing a speech about the importance of reading, repeat the word *reading* often. You can also repeat a phrase, such as, "Reading allows you to . . ." Here's an example from just after a hook:

First, reading allows you to learn more quickly. Second, reading allows you to get lost in your

Without words to follow along with, listeners may lose track of your main points.

imagination. And third, <u>reading allows you to</u> learn more about all school subjects.

It is good to repeat your main message so that listeners keep it in mind throughout your speech. If the main message is that reading is important, repeat this idea, even if you rephrase it:

From the very beginning of a child's life, he or she is taught that <u>reading is important</u>. First, reading allows you to learn more quickly. Learning plays a role in everything we do, from school to home to work. <u>Knowing how to read is critical</u> to a person's development.

Repeating words in a speech is like highlighting phrases in writing.

SAY IT AGAIN

Notice how the repeated words and phrases help highlight the main point in the following portion of a speech:

According to *Student Magazine*, 48 percent of children who don't get a 30-minute <u>recess</u> every day cannot catch their breath after one minute of running. Doctors who are experts on lungs suggest exercise as one way to stay fit. A <u>longer recess</u> is one way to exercise. Therefore, students should participate in a <u>longer recess</u> at school.

There are several advantages to a <u>longer recess</u>. One, it is a healthy choice for kids . . .

Quick Tips

- It is good to repeat yourself in a speech.
- Repeat key words or phrases.
- Restate your main message.

Consider Using Visuals

Studies have shown that most people learn visually. In other words, these people learn faster and better with things they can see. They do not learn as quickly or remember as long with only spoken words. Consider using visuals with your speech to help listeners understand your ideas. Photos, maps, and graphs are some examples of visuals.

If you have access to a computer, it might be easy to make a presentation to go with your speech. If so, make sure you include more visuals than words in the presentation. Visuals can be distracting if they are too complicated. And listeners will not be able to listen to your speech and read a screen at the same time. Instead, talk about your visuals in

Seeing examples can help listeners understand your speech.

Look at your audience when using visuals.

your speech. Guide your audience through them. If there are words on your visuals, say them for listeners. But if you do say something that also appears on the screen, make sure you keep your eyes on the audience. You do not want your listeners to feel as though you are talking to the screen. Make sure

to never turn your back on your listeners.

Finally, make sure your technology works and you know how to use it. If something goes wrong with the visual presentation during your speech, your listeners might feel awkward and get distracted.

TRY IT OUT

Write down ideas: What photos could you use? Are there any graphs that would help support your idea? What other visuals would help your speech?

Quick Tips

- Consider using visuals.
- Make sure the visuals support your speech.
- Even if you use visuals, keep your eyes on your listeners.

The End Is the Beginning

Your speech is coming to a close. You've engaged the crowd. You've given your main points. You now need to end your speech, and you need to end it well. A strong ending is one of the things listeners will remember. It will be the last thing they hear you say. It is the beginning of listeners reflecting on what you said.

The end is the time to tie things together. First, summarize your main points. Then, leave the listener with something to think about after your speech is done. You can end

Listeners may have questions at the end of your speech.

Quick Tips

- Write a strong ending that emphasizes your message.
- Save your best question, anecdote, or statistic for last.
- Motivate listeners to act on or think more about the new information you gave.
- Use fact and emotion in the ending.

TRY IT OUT

Write at least three ways to end your speech. Read your entire speech with each ending. Which is the strongest?

the speech with another question, anecdote, or statistic. Save the best one for last. You can also use your ending to call listeners to action. Or, you can tie things together by restating an opposing viewpoint.

You can then retell why your view is better.

Whichever way you choose to end your speech, make sure it includes both facts and emotion. Suppose your speech is about doing community service. It could end with, "Studies show that 90 percent of students who help in their community grow up to help in their communities as adults. Don't break the hearts of future communities!"

FINISHING STRONG

Statistics can make a strong ending:

Recess is a healthy activity for kids. It helps them burn off extra energy so they can focus in class. And it helps kids make friends and be more social. Forty-eight percent of children who don't get a 30-minute recess have a hard time catching their breath. According to *Student Magazine*, 95 percent of them grow up with health issues. Let's stomp out this statistic with a longer recess and get kids healthier, happier, and smarter!

Shorten Your Speech

When Edward Everett gave his speech on November 19, 1863, in Gettysburg, Pennsylvania, it lasted more than two hours. The speech was more than 13,000 words long. President Abraham Lincoln then gave his speech. It was only about 250 words long and took two minutes. Whose speech is the most famous? Lincoln's short one. Write a short speech, not a long one.

Your speech is a time for you to tell others about your subject. But remember, you are also using their time. Be considerate of your listeners. Include only the most

Abraham Lincoln's speech became known as the Gettysburg Address.

Good speakers practice before their presentations.

important information about your subject. Your listeners will appreciate your putting in the extra work of shortening your speech. They will be more likely to reward you with their attention.

You may be given a word count or a time limit for your speech. If you have a time limit, take breaks as you write to read over what you've written. Time how long it takes for you to read it. Maybe your speech is supposed to be five minutes long. If it takes you three minutes to get through your first main point, you may need to use fewer details.

Having only a short time to keep listeners engaged means you must focus. Focus on your message. Focus on your ideas. Support your ideas.

Quick Tips

- Write a short speech.
- Focus on your message.
- Support your ideas.
- Write your speech in an organized way.

23

Practice, Practice, Practice

It's done! You've written your speech! Now it's time to practice giving the whole thing.

First of all, read it to yourself silently. How does it sound? Is there anything you want to change? Is it organized? Does it have transitions? Do you repeat key words and your main message? Does the end have fact and emotion?

The next time, read it out loud. Ask yourself the same questions as

Read your speech both silently and aloud.

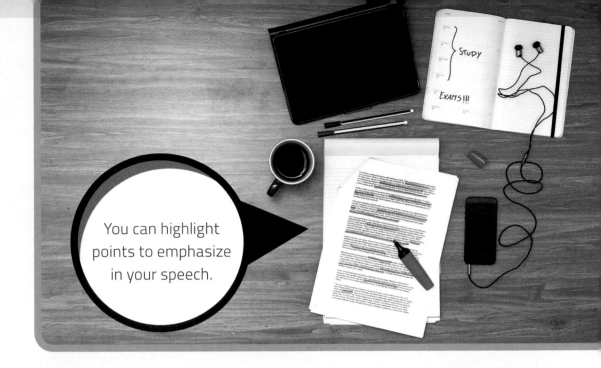

You can highlight points to emphasize in your speech.

when you read it silently. Change your words as needed. When you read it aloud a second time, make marks on your paper. Decide where you should read more loudly or with more enthusiasm. You can underline these words. Maybe there's an important fact you want everyone to hear. You can write *S* for "stop," *P* for "pause," or *B* for "take a breath" just before this fact. Mark the notes in your own special way. It may look something like this:

"It is important to have science lessons every day. A boy named Cory had 30 minutes of science a day. He grew up to be [S] an astronaut."

Finally, with your marked-up script and any visuals, practice in front of others, even if it is only one person. Change your marks when needed. Change your words as you see fit. Then, practice some more.

Quick Tips

- Read your speech out loud and silently.
- Note on your paper ways you want to say things.
- Practice in front of people.

Deliver Your Speech

It's time to deliver your speech. There are several things to remember when giving your speech.

First, keep your posture straight. Keep your shoulders rolled back. Stand tall and proud. This will help you breathe more easily and make you look more confident. Second, make sure you speak at the right volume. You've practiced your speech out loud. But maybe now you are in a larger room. You might even be speaking through a microphone. Make sure your voice is loud enough so that everyone can hear you but without hurting the ears of the people closest to you. Third, don't forget to make eye contact. Your

Pay attention to how loudly you speak through a microphone.

listeners want to connect with you. Look all around and catch people's eyes. Avoid filler words, such as *um* and *uh*. You've practiced your speech already, so you should be set to go.

Because you might be nervous, you might start talking quickly. If this happens, take a deep breath and slow down. You want to make sure you are speaking slowly enough for others to hear all of what you are saying.

Finally, use body movements to connect with listeners. Walk back and forth. Make hand gestures.

Quick Tips

- Keep your posture straight.
- Speak in a strong voice that is not too loud.
- Remember to keep eye contact and use gestures.
- Avoid filler words.
- Speak slowly.

Standing motionless looks and feels awkward. It might distract listeners from what you have to say.

When you're finished, thank your listeners for listening. They might thank you with a round of applause!

Make sure to thank your listeners for their time.

Writer's Checklist

✓ Choose a topic you want to focus on.

✓ Keep it simple. Focus on one main message.

✓ Think about who your audience will be.

✓ Hook the listener with the beginning of the speech.

✓ Choose words you can say easily.

✓ Guide the listener with structure and transitions.

✓ Repeat key words, phrases, and ideas.

✓ Consider using visuals to help listeners follow along.

✓ End your speech with fact and emotion.

✓ Keep your speech short.

✓ Practice your speech silently and out loud.

✓ Speak loudly enough so everyone can hear.

Glossary

anecdote
A story about an interesting event.

cardinal numbers
Numbers used in counting, such as *one*, *two*, and *three*.

formal
Following an established form or set of rules.

gesture
A movement that emphasizes an idea or a feeling.

lectern
A stand with a slanted top that a speaker can read off.

opposing
Opposite or in conflict with.

ordinal numbers
Numbers that indicate position in a series, such as *first*, *second*, and *third*.

posture
The position of a person's body.

statistic
A number that represents a piece of information.

tone
The feeling or attitude expressed by someone.

tongue twister
A sequence of words that are hard to pronounce correctly.

visual
Something to look at that makes an idea easier to understand.

For More Information

Books

Bodden, Valerie. *Classroom How-To: How to Write a Research Paper*. Mankato, MN: The Creative Company, 2015.

Fields, Jan. *You Can Write Excellent Reports*. Mankato, MN: Capstone Press, 2012.

Jakibiak, David. *Smart Kid's Guide to Doing Internet Research*. New York: Rosen Publishing Group, 2009.

Minden, Cecilia, and Kate Roth. *How to Write and Give a Speech.* North Mankato, MN: Cherry Lake Publishing, 2011.

Visit 12StoryLibrary.com

Scan the code or use your school's login at **12StoryLibrary.com** for recent updates about this topic and a full digital version of this book. Enjoy free access to:

- Digital ebook
- Breaking news updates
- Live content feeds
- Videos, interactive maps, and graphics
- Additional web resources

Note to educators: Visit 12StoryLibrary.com/register to sign up for free premium website access. Enjoy live content plus a full digital version of every 12-Story Library book you own for every student at your school.

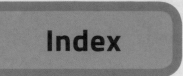

Index

About the Author

Catherine Elisabeth Shipp is a writer and a teacher who has published more than a dozen children's books, with more on the way. She lives with her husband and twins in Minnesota.

READ MORE FROM 12-STORY LIBRARY

Every 12-Story Library book is available in many formats. For more information, visit 12StoryLibrary.com.